BLOGGING MADE SIMPLE

Powerful Strategies for Blogging Success

By Michael H. Fleischner
Justin Freid

Michael Fleischner

Dedicated to Jamie, Samantha, Alex- My inspiration and joy

To my father, brother, and extended *family*

In memory of my mother

Justin Freid

To my parents, Jay and Melinda Freid, for teaching me that if you want something, the only way to get it is through hard work.

Contents

Chapter 1

Introduction

Welcome to the world of blogging. As someone who's been blogging for a number of years, I can share how incredibly rewarding it can be as both a full-time venture and hobby. Its benefits are virtually endless. Each day millions of people read blogs for information or post content to their own blogs as part of their daily routine. Blogging is everywhere, and learning the fundamentals of effective blogging is within your reach.

If you don't have your own blog, rest easy. Justin and I will show you how to get started quickly and put yourself on the path to successful blogging. If you've been blogging for a while but want to learn more about building a following or profiting from your posts, we'll show you how to do that as well. Regardless of your starting point, this book is designed to help you take your blogging to the next level. It uses real-world examples and provides practical how-to advice you won't find anywhere else.

Blogging is a rewarding experience for those who want to fully leverage one of the most powerful online communication platforms available today. In over a decade of blogging and doing business online, I've learned that having an Internet presence can significantly impact what you do online and off-line. Some people blog for fun; for others, it's a full-time job. Whether you're blogging for profit, looking to start a movement, or building your online reputation, learning effective blogging techniques is the best place to start.

My primary blog, "The Marketing Blog" (http://marketing-expert.blogspot.com), is the number-one marketing blog online. That's a pretty bold claim, but with the number-one ranking on Google among more than 1.05 billion search results, I know my blog is special. "The Marketing Blog" generates thousands of daily page views and unique visitors every day. Imagine what *you* could do with that kind of traffic. I'm always looking for and experimenting with new ways to leverage my blog traffic to meet my personal and professional goals.

Since launching my blog a number of years ago, I've learned a great deal about creating blogs that people find valuable. In this guide we'll show you how generate valuable content and improve your overall ranking and popularity. We'll also show you how to attract loyal followers to your blog every day. This is essential for building a reputable site that others want to emulate.

As a result of my blog's popularity, I've experienced a significant number of benefits in my professional career. I wish I could say I would have experienced these benefits without the blog, but it's undeniable that having an effective platform for communicating, connecting with others, and building an online reputation has significantly helped me acquire speaking engagements, consulting opportunities, moneymaking partnerships, and much more. I hope that makes you excited, because no matter what your specific goals are, building a successful blog is really easy to do and we're going to show you how.

In addition to "The Marketing Blog," I've launched and managed other blogs for myself and for several small- to medium-sized businesses that wanted to expand their online presence. The experience I've gained has helped me continually improve my own blogs and use them as a springboard for other business ventures such as affiliate marketing and online publishing. Once you start blogging, you'll quickly discover dozens of ways to earn a passive income. I love blogging. The fact that I can make a nice living doing it is just icing on the cake.

As someone who's authored a number of how-to guides for those seeking information about online marketing (*SEO Made Simple*, *Article Marketing Made Simple*), my goal is to provide you with actionable information and ensure that you get the maximum benefit from this book. *Blogging Made Simple* is designed to provide you with step-by-step instructions for setting up and starting your own blog—whether you're looking to share your thoughts online, support a business, or earn a profit.

To provide you with the most powerful blogging advice and give you a variety of options to choose from when setting up and running your blog I've teamed up with my longtime friend and business partner Justin Freid to write this book. I approached Justin with the idea of collaborating on the subject because he is what I call "tuned in." If you haven't heard of Justin, he's popular in social media circles and is a great blogger and Internet marketer with a lot of experience using popular blogging platforms. Together we'll teach you everything you need in order to meet your blog-related goals and objectives. The advice we offer is based on real-world experiences, not on academic theory or useless musings. We don't want you to waste your time struggling to set up a blog or dealing with trivial issues. Rather, our goal is to minimize the challenges commonly associated with launching and maintaining a blog and get you focused on leveraging everything it has to offer. Our primary goal is to help you realize the specific outcomes you want most.

Not Sure if Blogging Is for You?

From my perspective, blogging is the best way to share your ideas and communicate with like-minded people online. It's also a great way to earn a passive income. For many in the blogging community, having a blog is about earning money or supporting a growing business in a way that doesn't take a lot of time or effort. Whether you're looking to share your ideas or turn a profit, blogging can be your key to success.

Successful bloggers are people who enjoy sharing their ideas with others. They spend time writing in-depth posts about particular topics, lend their expertise, focus on building a community, and continually reinvent themselves. But don't let the full scope of running a successful blog scare you. If your time is limited, you can still take advantage of the techniques we reveal in this guide, including outsourcing many of your blog-related tasks for as little as three bucks an hour. Effective outsourcing allows you to develop and maintain a very successful blog with minimal effort and expense. However, if you think blogging is about worthless rants or repurposed content, think again. Successful bloggers know the precise formula for creating quality content, building strong followers, and monetizing their visitors through a variety of techniques. The best bloggers make their experience a win-win for both their audience and themselves.

Quality content is something we'll mention often in this guide. If you want your blog to rank high on major search engines and wish to build a large list of followers, then you'll need to offer your audience powerful, engaging content that provides real value. Think about the websites or blogs you currently read. Do they provide information in a way that engages you? They must create value or you wouldn't read them or return. The most successful blogs are significant to more than just you. They also generate value for others who share similar interests. Reaching large social networks with your blog is essential for success. The lines between blogging and social media have become somewhat blurred in recent years. This is good news for bloggers like me who leverage social media to drive traffic to my blog.

During our journey together, you may find similarities among social media, blogging, and microblogging. With the advent of free applications that integrate social media outlets such as Facebook, Twitter, and Google+ directly into blogging platforms, sharing your content across the Internet has never been easier. We'll touch on the subjects of social media and microblogging (for example, Twitter) but focus most of our discussion on blogging itself. Social media plugins are evolving so rapidly that attempting to cover all of them here would be meaningless. However, you should keep in mind that all successful blogs effectively leverage real-time content in the form of social media. Each of the blogging platforms we cover in this book has made integrating social media extremely easy to do. We'll show you how to add your tweets, Facebook posts, and other social communications directly into your blog. This provides frequent updates and engaging content for your readers with little effort. The timeliness and frequency of your updates also help with search engine optimization.

You Are Not Alone

The concept of blogging was studied a great deal when it was first introduced, but less so more recently as the novelty has worn off. This is largely due to the influence of microblogging, but things are coming full swing now that blogging and microblogging are becoming more integrated. One source, Technorati, a popular online blog catalog, has conducted some very helpful research in the form of annual surveys administered to the blogging community that give insight into blogging and the types of people who blog successfully.

According to last year's survey by Technorati there are four primary categories of bloggers:

Hobbyist. These individuals represent the majority of bloggers who are casual contributors. Their motivation for blogging is enjoyment, not financial gain, branding, or other purposes. Content is largely focused around personal issues or concerns.

Part-Timer. This category describes bloggers who spend a significant portion of their time blogging (more than three hours per week). The motivation for these individuals goes beyond personal issues and blogging helps supplement their income.

Corporate: This was the smallest group identified by the Technorati study (Penn Schoen Berland, 2010). Individuals in this category blog full-time but don't use it as their only source of income. Many people blog to share their expertise with others in their niche.

Self-Employed: The final category includes those who blog full-time or occasionally for their own company or organization. Many own a company and have a blog related to their business. According to the study, self-employed individuals are the most likely to blog about business or professional topics.

Which Category Do You Fit Into?

As is true with any type of categorization, your blogging behavior may be a combination of more than one of these types. Regardless, you're reading this book because you are interested in blogging—and you've come to the right place. We'd like to simplify the blogging landscape and focus on *blogging for fun* and *blogging for business.* Why? If you're blogging for business (your own or someone else's) or pleasure, you'd better be having fun. It keeps you interested in producing new, quality content that engages your readers and helps you grow your online presence. It's also essential for making money. Trying to make money by promoting products that you would never use or have no interest in selling is like getting a root canal—it's no fun at all.

Blogging for Fun

Blogging is a great way to express yourself. People with unique hobbies all over the world create blogs to share their experience, artwork, and opinions on a wide variety of topics. It's a great way to communicate and attract like-minded individuals who share a passion for your specific hobby or niche.

So what should you start a blog about? Pretty much anything! If you're an avid photographer for example, you can create a blog that uses a portfolio-based theme to showcase your most recent work. Blogging is an effective way to share photographs with friends and family or others who are also interested in photography. If you love to travel, you can share information about your travels online. If you're planning an upcoming excursion or intend to go overseas for an extended period of time, you can log all of your pictures and memories on your blog. Blogging can help you stay connected with people back home who you'd like to keep updated on your adventures.

Staying in touch with family members and those interested in the same subject is another benefit of blogging. Long distances often separate people, and you may not be able to see your family or friends as much as you'd like. Starting a blog about your daily experiences will help keep you connected with others on a much larger scale than just speaking on the phone every few weeks. You can easily post pictures and hold conversations with your contacts, acquaintances, and family members using a well-designed blog.

For Justin and me, blogging is a way to be engaged with our passions. Whether we're blogging about search engine optimization, search marketing, social media, or any other Internet marketing topic, we're having a good time. What's great about having your own blog is that you attract others who share similar interests. You can expand your social network and gain knowledge and expertise.

Blogging should always be focused on a topic or idea you're passionate about. Without passion, you'll be one of the many who abandon their blogs and never reach the pinnacle of true blogging success. Focus on topics that drive you, whether for business or personal reasons. Blogging about something that you have an intimate knowledge about makes the process of updating your site much easier than if you're forced to write about a topic in which you have little or no interest. I know from personal experience that starting a blog on a topic you are not passionate about results in a blog that is left to wither on the vine. Create blogs about subjects that are important to you or your business.

Blogging for Business

Blogging to grow a personal business or company is a significant driver of the most recent blogging boom. Many individuals and corporations have discovered that blogging is an advertising and communications channel that has multiple benefits. Additionally, companies are using blogs to add content to their websites and attract repeat visitors. Whether you're a small mom-and-pop operation or a Fortune 500 company, blogging can help you interact with customers, increase sales, and rank higher in search engines.

Blogging opens up a significant communication channel for current and potential customers. By utilizing a blog correctly, companies gain the ability to discuss new business decisions, current events affecting their industry, and news concerning their products or services with interested parties. A blog can help customers stay up-to-date on what's happening with your brand and help you stay informed about how they feel about it. This is vital information that's difficult to find anywhere else. Blogging provides a unique platform for communicating with your target audience and building a sense of community.

The comments section of your blog can provide immediate feedback regarding your business. When customers find your newest product line exciting, the blog gives them a place to voice their opinion. If they don't enjoy your product, it provides an opportunity for you to gather feedback and understand why customers are unhappy. You can easily respond and interact with your clientele. Justin and I will show you how to utilize the comments feature inherent in blogs to manage user-generated content to improve the quality of the overall blogging experience.

Blogs are an essential part of the online buying experience. These days, consumers do a fair amount of research before making purchase decisions. They often use search engines to find information about companies and products. If your blog showcases the latest developments in your company and provides an interactive experience for customers, chances are you'll leave a positive impression, which can lead to sales.

One of the greatest benefits of blogging for business is the affect it has on search engine rankings. By producing quality content for visitors, search engines like Google and Bing are more likely to list your site high in their rankings. With recent updates to the Google algorithm, freshness of content has been elevated in importance. If your site integrates social media and is updated with quality content on a regular basis, Google increases the value of your blog and, in turn, your rankings.

As your blog climbs in search engine results, you will see an increase in traffic, leads, and sales. Ideally, you'll be able to convert these new visitors into loyal blog followers or paying customers, ultimately increasing your bottom line and growing your business. We'll show you specific techniques for building a powerful marketing list, one of the most valuable assets your blog can deliver. The marketing list is essential for anyone trying to generate revenue from a blog.

Justin and I use our blogs for much more than generating revenue. In fact, our primary purpose is to establish ourselves as experts in our industry and build credibility among our target markets. This allows us to grow our respective businesses and create value for our followers across a number of different platforms. Regardless of your goal, keep in mind that being focused on a particular topic—one that you're truly passionate about—really drives your blogging success.

What You Should Know about Blogging

According to the Technorati study mentioned earlier, about 95 percent of people who start blogs end up abandoning them. In fact, only 7.4 million of the more than one hundred million blogs being tracked had been updated in the previous one hundred and twenty days. Blog abandonment is not a new issue, and I'm even guilty of it myself.

Let's see why some people do not continue down the path to becoming a successful blogger. If you can address these pitfalls early on, you will be more likely to push your blog onto success.

- Some bloggers quit because the issue or event that motivated them to start blogging in the first place has faded away.

- Some quit blogging because of time constraints with work, family, or health.

- Some quit when they find out that blogging isn't the instant path to riches they thought it was.

- Some people do not update their blogs for months on end because they find it easier to use Twitter or another microblogging service.

Regardless of the obstacle, I encourage you to push forward. There will inevitably come a time when you wonder if the effort is worth the reward. Remember, with effort comes prestige, profit, and fulfillment. Consider why you started blogging in the first place. It's important to focus on what you want to blog about and establish short- and long-terms goals.

Blogging Statistics

In preparing to write this book, I found a number of interesting statistics about the blogging community. According to Jupiter Research, 57 percent of bloggers have a household income under $60,000 per year. When it comes to blog readers, Jupiter's figures show that blogs are primarily read by men (60 percent vs. 40 percent women) in households where the total income is over $60,000 per year.

My favorite statistics on blogging come from a study conducted last year by Technorati called the "State of the Blogosphere." It focused specifically on people who own and publish blogs. Based on the report:

- Technorati has indexed 1.33 million blogs since 2002.

- 346 million people globally read blogs.

- On average, 900,000 blog posts are published in a twenty-four-hour period.

- 77 percent of active Internet users read blogs.

- 55 percent of bloggers drink more than two cups of coffee per day.

- 81 languages are represented in the blogging community.

- 59 percent of bloggers have been blogging for at least two years.

- 49 percent of bloggers are based in the United States and 29 percent reside in Europe.

The report contends that the discipline of blogging is in a state of transition. It is no longer an upstart community. Bloggers' use of and engagement with social media tools is expanding and the lines between blogs, microblogs, and social networks have become blurred. As blogging converges with social media, posts are increasingly shared through social networks, even though blogs remain significantly more influential in terms of content.

According to the Technorati report, bloggers who earn revenue are generally blogging more this year than they were last. And 48 percent of bloggers believe that more people will get their news and entertainment from blogs than from traditional media in the next five years. The study asked consumers about their attitudes toward blogs and other media: 40 percent agreed with bloggers' views, and their trust in the mainstream media is declining.

The study was very interesting and you should definitely search online for Technorati's annual blogging surveys to stay up-to-date with the latest blogging trends.

Setting Goals

One of the most essential strategies to launching, building, and maintaining prominent blog is setting goals. If you're new to blogging, your goal might simply be to launch your site. If you have an established blog, your goal might be to generate $1,000 per month in ad revenue or grow your mailing list to a certain size. Regardless of the goal, it's important to have one.

When I first started blogging, my goal was to launch a site by a certain date. This motivated me to learn everything I could about different blogging platforms and how best to start a blog. I used every avenue available to plan and build my blog to achieve my goal. Once the site was up and running, I focused on creating quality content and set a goal of writing one quality post per week. That soon evolved into two or three posts per week, and eventually I took on guest posts from other experts in the marketing industry. The point I'm trying to make is that you should always operate under the premise of a specific, measurable goal. This practice has kept me going for years and continues to create ongoing profit and success.

I encourage you to start this journey by jotting down your top three blog-related goals on a sheet of paper. Your goals should be specific. For example, "Launch a blog by June 30." I know it sounds simple, but having a goal that you look at every day increases your chances of achieving it. Additionally, don't make the mistake I made when I first began setting goals. My first one was to make a million dollars with my blog the same year I launched it. Although it may have been a worthwhile aim, it wasn't until I started focusing on smaller, more tangible objectives that I saw real success. Don't abandon your dream of making however much money you want to acquire, but add supportive targets that can help get you there.

Once you've recorded your goals and posted them where you can see them on a daily basis, it's time to get started. Next we discuss popular blogging platforms.

Chapter 2

Blogging Platforms

Over the past few years, as blogging has become more popular, a number of platforms and tools have been developed to support their creation and management. Thank goodness—without them, blogging would not be nearly as easy or as lucrative. Whether you're building a blog as an integral part of your business or creating your own personal site for fun, platforms such WordPress, Blogger, and Tumblr make blogging quite simple. Each platform has pros and cons. Before you launch your blog, it's best to determine which one will help you meet your specific blogging goals.

Blogging platforms have evolved dramatically in recent years. From my perspective there isn't any reason to build a blog without using one of these tools. Developers are continually adding new features and improving usability, making the thought of creating and managing a blog through customized programming seem ridiculous.

People often ask me which platform I use. Unfortunately the answer to that question is complex because I use all of them for different reasons. Determining what suits your needs really comes down to understanding the strengths and weaknesses of each. Once you've determined what you'll be blogging about and what you want your blog to achieve, it will be easier to select the right platform. Let's begin with a basic overview of blog platforms and then explore each one in more depth.

Blogger

Blogger is owned and operated by Google. Since I'm partial to Google, I started my own blogs on the Blogger platform. Much like WordPress, the platform allows for the addition of widgets and offers some design flexibility for customizing your blog's look and feel. Widgets are plugins or additional modules that can be added to your blog to give you more features and functionality.

For example, you might add a social media widget that allows you to connect your Facebook fan page to your blog. Followers can "like" your fan page and post comments using this widget. Blogger doesn't provide a huge variety of social media plugins, but it has all the basics covered. You can add additional widgets to accommodate advertising, RSS feeds, and much more. Plugins are a great way to enhance your blog and improve the overall experience for visitors.

Blogger also offers a variety of design templates. To adjust your layout, you can simply add modules and move their location by dragging them to the appropriate region on your webpage. Additionally, if you want a truly unique design, you can use HTML code to create a custom layout. It may take some time to get your blog looking exactly the way you want it to, but you'll get there. Keep tweaking and experimenting.

Blogger is a very stable platform and I like its simplicity. The same can be also said for WordPress and Tumblr, though. Blogger is a great option for those who want to get started quickly and are looking for basic options.

WordPress

WordPress is one of the leading platforms, and it supports some of the largest blogs in the United States. It is a one-stop shop for businesses and individual bloggers who want to set up and run a blog independently or as an integrated feature of their websites. We'll teach you how to start a WordPress blog and discuss hosting options later in the chapter. Don't let the thought of hosting your blog scare you. Setting up a WordPress site is easy and hosting provides a number of benefits over traditional blogging platforms.

Although most platforms provide a hosting solution—meaning you create an online account and manage everything via the Web—WordPress offers a second solution that allows you to host a site on your own server. The benefit of hosting a blog on your own Web server is that it gives you complete control. If you use a hosted which is common with most platforms, you are subject to the rules and regulations of the host provider. They can do whatever they want with your blog; it can be banned or removed at any time without notice.

Don't panic. I've been working with hosted and self-hosted solutions for years and have never had any major problems. The one occasion when I had a small issue, it was quickly resolved. Rather than worry about hosting, focus on the benefits associated with each blog platform and choose the one that works for you.

WordPress is feature-rich and offers a wide range of design templates. In fact, because of its popularity, many third-party sites offer templates you can use to make your blog look very professional. Another benefit associated with WordPress is the large number of plugins available. From search engine optimization (SEO) to content updates, WordPress has it all.

Tumblr

Tumblr claims to be the Internet's leading microblogging platform. With more than ten billion posts, it has surpassed WordPress in page views and revenues. The Tumblr platform is considered to be a movement toward "light" blogging and is used by a number of leading brands to drive users to their websites.

One unique feature of Tumblr is the ability to report content from other Tumblr blogs. This functionality is similar to what you would find on Pinterest and other "repost" type platforms. I consider Tumblr to be a microblogging solution because it is often used by individuals looking to make small but frequent updates that incorporate multimedia.

No matter which platform you choose, you'll be glad to know that developing a blog is easy on all of them. These platforms are recognized by search engines and allow effortless management of content.

How Do You Decide?

In my experience, one of the most important aspects of blogging is determining whether you plan to host the blog on your own server. As mentioned, Blogger and Tumblr are solutions where the provider is hosting for you. As a result, you're at the mercy of the platform and subject to its rules and regulations. Even though using a third-party platform does carry an element of risk, I've been using Blogger for more than five years and have only had one small issue that was quickly resolved. Using a platform-hosted solution gives you immediate access to features that would otherwise have to be developed from scratch.

If you determine that your blog should be hosted on your own website, then WordPress is the solution we recommend. On the other hand, if you are building and optimizing an independent blog with no plans to integrate it into a website, then WordPress.com, Blogger, or Tumblr are all excellent choices.

Setting up accounts on each of the platforms is very easy to do and only takes a few short minutes. As such, we strongly recommend that you register accounts to get a feel for each platform. Since the services are free, there's no risk and your only investment is time. Setting up accounts and publishing posts doesn't take long and will provide you with a good feel for the unique qualities of each platform.

I also recommend adding a few widgets, changing designs, and altering your layout once you've set up an account. Figure out how simple or difficult each platform is for you to use in terms of creating a look and feel you want. You don't have to build the perfect blog in thirty minutes, but you should be able to determine which system works best for you.

Once we've provided you with a more comprehensive look at each platform, you'll be better prepared to find the one that is appropriate to your blogging goals and objectives.

Chapter 3

Getting Started

You can create a blog about anything. However, you'll want to be selective about the name, URL, look, and feel of the site. The goal should be to stand out among other blogs in your niche. To be successful online, you really want to think about your unique value proposition and implement your positioning throughout your designs, posts, widgets, and other blog elements. Consider the following before you begin publishing with any blogging platform.

Choosing a Niche or Theme

A niche is a market segment or type of person you want to speak to. Some people know right away whom they are targeting and others need guidance. A great place to begin is with a general list of blog categories.

- Arts

- Business

- Education

- Entertainment

- Family

- Fashion

- Food and drink

- Gaming

- Health and wellness

- Humor

- Lifestyle

- Music

- News and media

- Personal development

- Personal journal

- Pets and animals

- Photography

- Politics

- Relationships

- Society and culture

- Spirituality

- Sports

- Technology

- Transportation

- Travel

- Writing

Once you have identified a broad category, work your way through your idea until you can define a segment that your blog will appeal to. For example, my blog caters to Internet marketing professionals. Even though my target seems broad, it really isn't. Most of my posts are geared toward marketers doing business online. I defined my target by starting with marketing and then narrowing my theme based on what I was most comfortable writing about.

Another example might be someone in the same space who wants to talk about social media. Their blog might target others who want to learn about Facebook, Twitter, Google+, and so on. By knowing who you're writing for, you can quickly and easily choose a name, URL, and design for your blog. If you aren't sure who your target is, these steps will be next to impossible. In fact, I've seen numerous blogs created—only to be taken down and started all over again. Why? The publisher didn't have a clear understanding of the audience he or she was trying to reach.

Choosing a Title

Before setting up your blog, you need to choose a name. WordPress provides is a free option that allows you to use your chosen name in the URL followed by "wordpress.com." For example, if we chose a title like, "BettysQuilts," the blog address would appear as www.bettysquilts.wordpress.com. You can upgrade your account to allow for a basic URL, such as

"BettyQuilts.com," for a small fee. A similar feature exists on Blogger that allows you to point a domain you own to where your blog is hosted. In either case, you'll need to brainstorm a few names. Keep in mind that there are already millions of blogs online. Don't be surprised if your first, second, or third name choices have already been taken. It helps to have a variety of names to select from before you begin.

Choosing a Layout

Each of the platforms we have discussed offers standard design templates. In recent years, the number and flexibility of templates have grown exponentially, and there are even sites dedicated to producing Blogger, WordPress, and Tumblr templates. That said it's a good idea to think about what kind of design will appeal to your audience. The best way to do this is by visiting blogs in your niche and making note of design features you find appealing and flexible enough to meet your needs.

Once you've thought about your target audience, name, URL, and design, you're ready to get started with the blog creation process. The good news about choosing a blogging platform is that they all provide viable options for building a powerful site. Blogger is great if you're into Google and looking for a solid solution with standard functionality. WordPress offers a huge number of plugins and additional features, and Tumblr is a quick and easy blogging solution.

As a next step, we will be giving you a closer look at each blogging platform. It's always a good idea to register for these sites and follow along as we lead you through the setup and review process. While working directly with each blogging platform, notice the features that appeal to you and determine which one you prefer working in. If you're going to be blogging for years to come, you want to find something that meets your needs and is easily managed.

Although we are starting with Blogger, don't misinterpret this as our preference. The reason we cover three primary blogging platforms is because they are the most popular and most robust. We use different platforms for different reasons and our intent is simply to give you enough information about each of them to make the decision that's right for you. Let's dive in and first take a look at Blogger.

Blogger

Blogger is a Google property. This means that you are required to have a Gmail account to log in with. Visit http://www.gmail.com to create a Gmail account from scratch. You can also use an existing Gmail account that you're already using. Once you have a gmail email address you can sign up for Blogger. Simply go to http://www.blogger.com and click on "Get started." The login screen should look something like this.

Once you've logged for the first time, Blogger will step you through the sign up process:

The first step is to choose a display name that includes your primary key word phrase—the phrase you want your blog to be associated with. Your display name will become your signature line for blog posts. For example, it could be "Betty Quilts" or "Marketing Guy." You may have to try a number of variations before you find an available name, but be persistent. Eventually you'll find one that is closely aligned with your key words and is available for a new account.

To secure your blog, you must verify your account. This can be done via text or voice. If you choose text, Google will send you a code via text message to be entered online. Once you have entered the code, you will be asked to add a blog title.

The final step is to choose a design template. You can change your template at any time, so don't feel as though you're making a commitment that can't be reversed. A wide range of templates are available for Blogger, or you could commission a custom design from an HTML expert.

Choose a design that accommodates the widgets and layout necessary to meet your blogging goals. For example, if you intend to have advertising on your blog, look for a design into which ads could easily fit. On the other hand, if your focus is social media, find something that allows for the integration of multimedia accounts. The idea is to choose a template that meets your immediate and long-term needs.

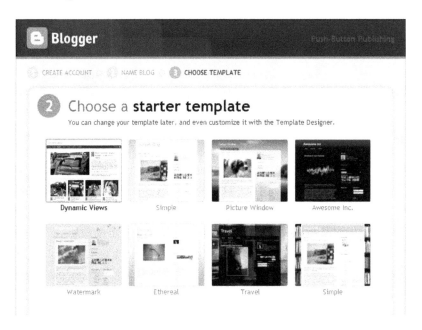

Now that you're through the sign-up and template selection process, you're ready to create your first post. Blogger's interface is a rich dashboard that displays all your blogs, offers statistics, and provides access to your posts and template.

The image below is a screenshot of the dashboard of one of my Blogger accounts.

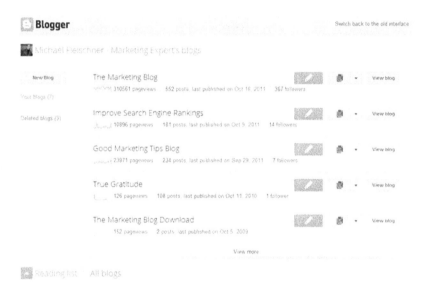

If you only have one blog in your account, it will be listed on your dashboard. To make your first post, click the orange button with the pencil icon. From there, it's as simple as creating a title and typing your entry.

The Marketing Blog · Post
Save   Preview   Close
Compose   HTML   ... J · ·T · B I U ABC A · · Link ... ... · · · · · · · · · · · · · · ·

· Post settings
Labels
Schedule
Location
Options

Make sure you create posts that contain unique content. Duplicate content negatively impacts search engine rankings and may turn off your intended audience. It's a good idea to include images, videos, and other multimedia to help engage readers. The next step is to add labels, a schedule, your location, and additional options.

Labels. Adding labels to your posts is important because doing so allows search engine spiders to categorize your content properly. More importantly, if users search your site for specific content, the right labels allow them to find what they're looking for quickly and easily. I like to label my posts with very specific key words. Don't use dozens of key words; a few highly targeted labels will do the trick.

Schedule. This feature enables your post to be published at some point in the future. If you write a post today and don't want it to go live until later in the week, you can choose the date and time it should be published. This is especially helpful if you write a number of posts in one sitting and want to spread them out over a week.

Location. The location feature is valuable for bloggers who cater to a local audience. If you want people to see where you are posting from, enter your location in the search box and press "Done." Blogger will attach your position to each post.

Options. The options tab gives you control over user comments and post composition. If you'd like users to be able to comment on your posts, click "Allow." I strongly recommend that you moderate your comments to avoid spam, which devalues your blog and undermines its credibility. Under "Compose mode," leave the "Interpret typed HTML" option selected.

The last option to select is "line breaks". If you set this option after your post has gone live, you can leave the selection alone. If you want to set it prior to posting, choose "Enter." In compose mode, pressing enter creates a text break to separate paragraphs.

When you're ready for your first post to go live, click "Publish," and it should appear on your home page. You can view and edit posts at any time from the dashboard.

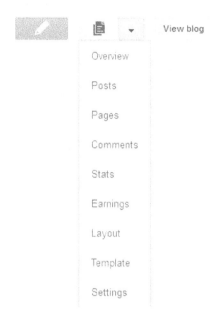

Advanced Features of Blogger

The good news is that even though the following features are considered advanced, they are easy to understand and use. Let's begin with navigation.

Top Navigation. There are a few buttons that are always present at the top of the Blogger interface. They allow you to access key features from any page.

- The Blogger icon brings you to your home screen.

- The pencil is used to start a new post.

- The page icon gives you access to site features.

- The view blog button opens your blog in the same window.

Overview. The overview tab is designed to provide a quick snapshot of your blog's most important factors: news, traffic, comments, posts, and so on.

The main screen gives you a quick overview of how your site is growing or changing. You can easily navigate to all the other tabs associated with your blog using the navigation menu on the left side of the page.

Posts. The posts page is where you'll be spending most of your time. From there, you can see your most recent posts and even those you created a long time ago. By hovering your mouse over any post title, you have the option to edit, view, or delete the post. This makes it very easy to manage all your posts from a single location.

Oddly enough you can't create a new post from the main area of this screen, but as noted earlier, you can always start a new post using the pencil icon in the top navigation. This feature is really designed to accommodate changes to existing posts.

Pages. This feature is used to create stand-alone pages. You may have the need to create individual pages that are accessible from the top navigation of your blog. The pages feature can make your blog look more like a website and makes the challenge of creating navigation menus very easy. With the ability to develop unique pages, you have more control over expanding your site's overall size and scope. Pages are a great way to introduce new content and monetize your blog (by adding a directory, selling merchandise, and so on).

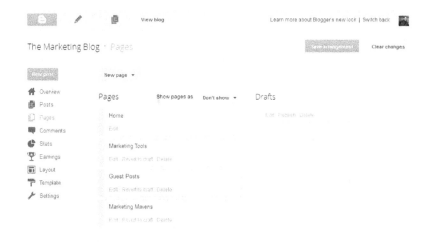

As you can see in the image above, each of the pages that appear in the top navigation of "The Marketing Blog" were added using the page feature of Blogger. I have easy access to add, edit, or delete these pages, which is essential for maintaining multiple pages on your blog.

Comments. Soon after you begin publishing posts and drawing attention to your blog, people will start leaving comments. User-generated content is important for any blog because it helps from a search engine optimization perspective and increases engagement. The comments section is where you can access and manage feedback from your visitors.

From the comments moderation section, you have access to comments you previously approved, those awaiting moderation, and those identified as spam.

Once you have set your blog for comment moderation, you must review each comment for approval, deletion, or markup as spam. One of the quickest and most effective ways to moderate comments is by deleting any that contain embedded links. These are often left by people looking for a free link and don't provide anything of value to your readers. I generally delete these comments or mark them as spam because I want to limit the number of outbound links I publish on my blog—a best practice when thinking about search engine optimization. You want more links that point to your blog rather than point out. The better your inbound-to-outbound-link ratio, the better your search rankings.

I'm pretty choosy about the comments I keep. What's fantastic about having your own blog is that you can determine which comments get published and which do not. I look for quality remarks that my blog readers will find value in. This encourages others to add to the conversation.

Something to note is that Blogger has a built-in spam detection system. As a result you may automatically find new listings under your spam tab. This is a good thing. If you had to evaluate all your comments individually to sort out the good ones from spam, you could waste quite a bit of time, especially as your blog traffic grows and you begin to receive dozens of comments each day.

Stats. This is one of my favorite tabs. Okay, I'm a sucker for numbers, but the stats page tells you everything you need to know about your blog traffic.

A graph on the stats tab shows the number of page views your blog has received over the previous week. On the right you'll see your page view stats for the day, the previous day, the previous month, and since inception.

The stats page also shows how many page views each post has received. I get excited when I see hundreds of views of my posts, and it gives me insight into the type of content my readers are most interested in.

The remaining sections show your traffic sources and audience information. Not only can you see which websites are sending you traffic, you can also click on "More" to view a complete list of top referrers. This is also true of the audience section.

Having one-click access to statistics of this nature is helpful for understanding your readers, determining which sites are generating traffic to your blog, and learning which key words are associated with your site.

Earnings. One easy way to make money with your blog is with the addition of AdSense. Google pays you each time someone clicks on an ad that appears on your site. If you're not familiar with AdSense, I encourage you to learn more. It's a great moneymaker and very easy to integrate with Blogger through the use of a widget.

The concept behind Adsense is quite simple – here's how it works. You display ads on your blog from the AdSense network. In essence you are selling ad space. However, Google handles finding and managing the advertisers for you. It requires next to no work on your part to display relevant ads to your blog readers because the entire process is automated. To set up your account, select the earnings tab.

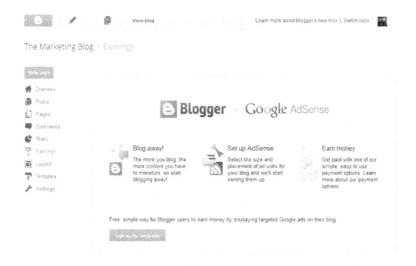

In the earnings section, enter your existing AdSense information to start displaying ads on your blog. If you do not have an AdSense account, you can quickly register for one through the Blogger interface. Once your registration is complete, you can display pay-per-click ads automatically. Incorporating AdSense into your blog is an easy way to earn income with very little effort. Be careful not to click on your own ads though. If you do, Google can close your AdSense account and ban you. This can be a tough pill to swallow, especially if you own and operate multiple blogs. Google is the largest online ad network, and being denied access to their platform can be a real drawback.

Layout. This is one of my favorite aspects of the Blogger interface. The layout section controls the overall organization of your blog. You can add, edit, and delete layout modules to create a truly customized blog that includes everything you want for building your business, generating revenue, or publishing content.

There are a number of areas in the Blogger interface where you can click the "Add a gadget" option. When you select this option, you're given a selection of gadgets you can add to your blog. One module I use frequently allows for the addition of JavaScript and HTML code, which opens the door to endless features and custom applications.

You can also edit or delete existing gadgets. Each gadget has an "Edit" link that provides access to the specific features that can be changed.

Gadgets can be moved or rearranged by dropping and dragging. What I love about this feature is that you can change the order and location of your widgets until you have a layout you're truly happy with.

Template. The layout section controls the modules that comprise your blog as well as its overall look and feel of your blog.

In the template section you can see a live view of your blog online and via mobile devices. When you click "Customize," your blog template can be changed with a single click (overall look, background, width, and so on). There are a number of templates to choose from, and you can preview each one before you apply any changes. I always try to preview changes before they are promoted. It provides an opportunity to see how your site will render once the customizations are live on the web.

The "Edit HTML" button provides access to the HTML code that drives your blog. Do not use this feature unless you have HTML experience or have worked with blog templates in the past. Before you do anything with your blog template, especially the HTML, back it up.

I've made a habit of backing up my template on a monthly basis. You can use an external hard drive or cloud-based storage to save a copy of your HTML code. Backing up your blog is a good habit to get into and one that has saved me on many occasions. If you are planning to implement any major changes to your blog, always start by copying your existing HTML template.

When you're working in this area to customize your blog or save your template, click on the "Expand widgets" check box to reveal all of the code associated with your blog. Leaving the box unchecked may hide some of your HTML, rendering some changes ineffective.

Settings. You can change many aspects of your overall blogging experience through the settings tab. You can set parameters for your blog's meta description and privacy, and even designate multiple authors. Click on a submenu item to access it and make appropriate changes.

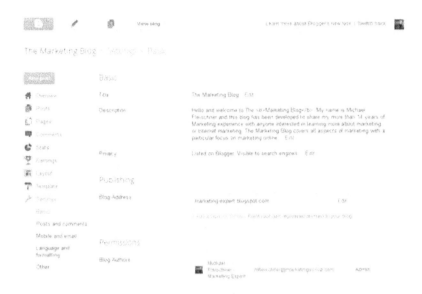

From the posts and comments area, you can identify how you would like posts and comments to appear, as well as designate your moderation settings. As noted earlier, I always enable content moderation. Doing so protects my blog against unwanted spam and gives me an opportunity to be selective about the user-generated content that appears on my site.

The next section controls mobile and e-mail settings. If you like to make short updates to your blog, you can post using SMS. Simply add your mobile device and start making posts from your phone. Your blog will update instantly. You could also enable comment notification e-mails so you are aware of comments awaiting moderation. If you access your blog on a regular basis, you probably don't need to set up e-mail notifications. Even though I access my site daily, I like getting the notifications as a reminder that I have posts waiting for moderation. Blogger allows you to approve or deny posts directly from the email, easing the process of content moderation.

The language and format setting controls the language and time stamp associated with your posts. Choose the language that you and your blog readers prefer. Then select the appropriate time settings and hit the "Save settings" button in the upper right corner of the screen to confirm your selections.

The final setting allows you to control other aspects of your blog. For example, you can delete your site, manage feeds, and add your Google Analytics ID.

Next Steps with Blogger

Now that we've covered all aspects of Blogger, you should be ready to build your site. After you've thought about your audience, decided on a name, and considered some of the features you'd like to include, start the registration process. Set up your blog the way you want it, and keep in mind that blogs are living, changing things. You always have the ability to add, delete, and change modules. Over the years, I've updated my blog hundreds of times—not just in terms of content, but also features, designs, and so on. It's part of expanding and growing your blog and is one of the most rewarding aspects of blogging.

WordPress

WordPress is one of the most popular content management systems available. Its easy-to-use interface has enabled small business owners and those who want to blog as a hobby the tools necessary for building a functional, great-looking blog or website.

WordPress is open source software, which means that developers from all over the world can create themes and plugins for everyone to use on the platform. Themes and plugins can help you personalize the design of your blog easily and are relatively easy to install.

WordPress is PHP- and MySQL-based, but don't worry about the need for programming or computer language experience. You can drag and drop widgets and plugins without touching any code. The dashboard is simple enough for someone with only a small background in website management to use, but contains enough flexibility for even the most creative website designer. Technically advanced blog owners can easily alter and update custom style sheets to create sites that are both unique and aesthetically pleasing. This level of control and customization makes blogging with WordPress fun and exciting. Many WordPress users start with a common theme and customize it to their liking.

Matt Mullenweg launched WordPress on May 27, 2003. Since then, it has grown exponentially and is now the content management system of choice for millions of bloggers and website developers. One of the major reasons WordPress is so popular is because it is open source. By taking this route, its creators inspired thousands of code hounds and developers to create themes, plugins, and improvements.

WordPress.com versus WordPress.org

WordPress is available in two different versions. One is hosted on WordPress servers and is found at Wordpress.com. The second version which is open source software can be found at WordPress.org.

There are certain advantages and disadvantages to each version. For those who blog as a hobby and want to write quick posts and upload pictures, the WordPress.com version is the best choice. Your URL will look something like this: http://www.myblog.wordpress.com.

An advantage to this type of hosting is that you do not have to pay a hosting service such as GoDaddy or HostGator. You also don't have to purchase a domain.

While these are great features, this version does have a few limitations. Because your site is hosted on WordPress.com's servers, you are limited as to the amount of information and data you can store. This caps the amount of customization you can have on your blog. If you use WordPress.com, you can choose a standard theme and alter things like color and font. You are also limited as to which plugins can be installed on your blog.

If you are more technically advanced and are looking to customize your blog or set up a small business website, WordPress.org is your best option. Once you have signed up with a web host and purchased your domain, you can easily install WordPress though your host control panel. Host providers often offer easy, automated WordPress installation and provide many features that make common tasks like buying a domain name or hosting your blog fairly straightforward.

There are quite a few advantages to working with WordPress.org. One is the ability to choose from thousands of themes available for download, and another is the many third-party plugins on the market you can use to enhance the functionality, look, and feel of your blog. Many theme templates can be downloaded for free, and there are an incredible number of premium themes available for purchase. These themes often have dashboards that allow for further customization. Look for one that offers the features that are important to you and upload it into WordPress to create your customized site.

There may be a small learning curve involved in uploading a custom template to your blog. However, most sites that offer WordPress templates provide written or video instructions on how to install your new theme. It's worth finding a theme that works for you. Spending some extra time on the setup is worth the gratification you will get from building a blog you are proud of.

Blog or Website?

WordPress is a great platform for creating and managing a blog, and it can also be useful for building a small business website. WordPress is so flexible that you can dictate whether your home page is a blog or a static page that contains information about your business. This aspect can be altered in the settings panel. You can also create custom layouts for your home page, other pages on the site, and blog posts. If you plan to build a blog for your small business, you can easily create a landing page that contains information about the business and a secondary page that displays your latest blog posts. A blog is an effective way to grow your website and interact with customers on a frequent basis. You might also want an About Us or Contact Us page.

Naming Your Blog

When choosing a name for your blog, keep the following in mind.

1. Your title should be SEO-friendly.

2. It should tell visitors what the site is about.

3. Your brand name should appear in the title.

What constitutes an SEO-friendly title? Well, think of it from a searcher's perspective. If someone using a search engine were looking for a company or resource in your industry, what would they type into the search field?

For example, let's say you're a plumber in Philadelphia. It is likely a Philadelphia resident with a burst pipe will head to Google, Yahoo!, or Bing to search for "plumbers in Philadelphia" or "Philadelphia plumbers." You would be well advised to include some variation of "plumbers in Philadelphia" in your site's title. This will help your chances of appearing in search results and encourage users to click through. WordPress uses the title of your blog as the title tag (<title>) of your website, which is useful for search engine rankings. Keep in mind, though, that it is just one of many factors involved in search engine optimization.

You can easily edit the title of your website under the settings tab in WordPress. In the image below, you can see where to enter your SEO-friendly title.

Site Title	Enter Site Name Here	
Tagline	Enter Branded Tag Line Here	in a few words, explain what this site is about
WordPress Address (URL)	http://www.webaddress.com	
Site Address (URL)	http://www.webaddress.com	Enter the address here if you want your site homepage to be different from the directory you installed WordPress
E-mail Address	email@gmail.com	This address is used for admin purposes, like new user notification.
Membership	☐ Anyone can register	
New User Default Role	Subscriber ▾	
Timezone	UTC+0 ▾	UTC time is 2012-04-01 21:25:14
	Choose a city in the same timezone as you.	
Date Format	◉ April 1, 2012	
	○ 2012/04/01	
	○ 04/01/2012	
	○ 01/04/2012	
	○ Custom F j, Y April 1, 2012	
	Documentation on date and time formatting.	

If you are not a business and have a blog set up for your hobby or personal interest the title of your blog is still important. Suppose you have a stack of delicious cookie recipes and would like to post them online. Make sure the title of your blog includes key words that a potential visitor might enter in a search engine.

To attract recipe hunters, you might title your blog "Aunt May's Delicious Cookie Recipes" or "Easy Cookie Recipes for the Busy Mom." Not only are these titles branded, but they also contain key words that potential visitors are likely to type into a search engine. Use the Google AdWords Keyword Tool to determine actual search volumes of popular key words and phrases in the Google search engine.

Navigating WordPress

From the WordPress dashboard, you can create a new page, write new blog posts, change the theme of your blog, and add different plugins and widgets. A navigation pane appears in the left sidebar of the WordPress interface. Below we explain each section in the pane.

Posts. The post tab lets you create new blog posts. When the tab is expanded, options appear for creating a new post, managing your current posts, or editing categories and post tags. Categories and post tags group your blog posts together. For example, if you have a home improvement blog, you may have posts on tools, gardening, and window and door installation. You can separate these posts into categories so that your readers can find them easily. If some posts fit into multiple categories, you can use post tags for further grouping. This helps keep your blog organized and your content easily accessible.

The "Add new" link will take you to a page that allows you to create a new blog post. The intuitive layout will guide you to insert a title for your post and start writing content. You can schedule when you would like your post to be published by selecting your preferred time and date.

Always post original content. Google and other search engines reward sites that produce fresh, original content on a regular basis. We recommend that you generate posts of three hundred or more words. The longer your posts, the more "spider food" you provide for search engines. Unique, key word–rich content is one of the reasons that blogs have become so powerful in search engine results.

Media. The media tab is where you can upload videos, pictures, and other media. You will be directed to upload files to your library, which can later be used in posts and pages. Think of this section as a parking lot. Your assets will be stored in the lot until you are ready to use them.

Links. If you have other blogs or websites or know someone who does, you may want to link to those sites. The "Add a link" button requests the anchor text and URL to create the link, which will appear wherever you place the widget. This improves the search results for the blogs or websites you link to and provides valuable resources for your visitors.

Pages. The pages tab is similar to the posts tab. Here you can add new pages and edit existing ones. Creating a page is straightforward and follows the same format as creating a post. The only difference is that the content won't be published as a post but will appear on a separate page. This is a great way to customize your blog, and it allows for meaningful, top-level pages that you can control.

You can do pretty much anything with individual pages. You might want an About Us or Contact Us page, or you could develop a page dedicated to selling merchandise. The possibilities are endless.

Comments. As you build traffic, you may find that people want to interact with your blog, and chances are that they will use comments to do so. Below the comments tab is a list of the latest comments left on your site. You can approve or edit them, or mark them as spam.

By determining which content is published or deleted, you directly control the user-generated content that appears on your site. As mentioned, it is always a good idea to moderate comments.

Appearance. The appearance tab is one of the most important tabs in the WordPress interface. This section allows you to upload new themes, change the order of the widgets on your pages, and alter menus.

Themes are really just different skins that allow you to edit the look and feel of your blog. Some even allow for extra customization. Many are available for free, but more advanced, customizable themes usually come at a cost.

Widgets let you make small changes that customize your site even further. Different themes come with different widgets, but the standard ones include a blogroll (a simple list of websites), a latest posts widget (highlighting the last few posts you created), categories (themes for your posts), and tag clouds (showing the most frequent tags associated with your posts).

You can also use menus to customize your WordPress site. Most themes include a navigation menu that allows you to show links at the top of your home page. You can pick and choose which pages or sections appear in the main navigation. This is a great feature for keeping blog followers focused on your most important pages.

Plugins. Plugins are one of the best things to happen to website building in quite some time! Thanks to the open source model of WordPress, developers can build add-ons that help your website perform better and improve the experience for your visitors.

For example, you may want to understand how people arrive at your site and what they do when they get there. To do so, you need an analytics program. One of the most popular programs is Google Analytics. There are plugins available that automatically tag your blog pages with Google Analytics code.

Other plugins help with search engine optimization (SEO), disabling comments, add name and e-mail capture forms, and incorporate social media.

Click on the plugin section in the navigation bar and select "Add new plugin." The page that loads will prompt you to search for your desired function. It's as easy as choosing a plugin and clicking "Install." Plugins allow you to continually expand your blog, and you can replace old widgets with new ones at any time.

Plugins give even the most novice website builder the ability to do things that only an experienced web developer could do in the past.

Users. The users tab allows the administrator to give or remove access to users of WordPress. It also gives you the ability to create and edit your profile.

If your site has more than one contributor, it is easier to manage if each person has individual log-in information.

Settings. In this section, you can manipulate the settings for your website or blog, such as selecting your home page and choosing the number of posts that will appear. Plugins are also listed here and can be easily edited.

Analytics

One of the most important things you can do to improve your blogging experience is to install an analytics program. WordPress offers a number of plugins for data capture and analysis. Analytics are an essential part of any blog – regardless of platform. Analytics programs track visitors to your site and tell you where they navigated, how much time they spent reading an article, and if they made a purchase or signed up for your newsletter. The most commonly used analytics tool is Google Analytics.

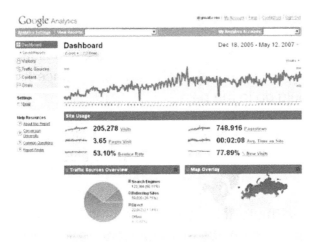

Google Analytics is free and can be easily installed on almost any website. In fact, there are plugins available that will automatically install Google Analytics for you.

Blogger, WordPress, and Tumblr have different analytics tools, but the important takeaway is that you should be paying attention to them.

By tracking how many people visit your site, how they got there, and what they did on it, you can better customize their experience. If you have a specific action you'd like your site visitors to complete, such as making purchases or signing up for a newsletter, you can see what hurdles are in their way. You can easily tell which page most people leave your site from and which content your visitors find most interesting. Use this information to make sure your site visitors complete the action you are hoping they will.

WordPress Safety

As we mentioned, WordPress is one of the most popular content management systems available, and unfortunately some people take advantage of it. If you utilize WordPress, it's important to update your software frequently. When you log in, you will be notified if there is an update available. It's a simple click to begin the upgrade process, and keeping your version up to date can prevent your site from being hacked or damaged in any way.

Plugins should be updated as well. Indicators will appear in the navigation of your dashboard to alert you when updates are available. Make the appropriate upgrades with just a few clicks.

If you do not keep your WordPress version and plugins up to date, you run the risk of your site being infected with malware, which can affect all websites on your server and those who visit your site. It's also a good idea to change your password frequently. Use a combination of numbers and letters for maximum protection.

Tumblr

Getting started with Tumblr is also very easy to do. At http://www.tumblr.com you will be prompted to provide an e-mail address, password, and your URL of choice. The URL will end in ".tumblr" and, for search engine optimization, you may want to include targeted key words within your domain name.

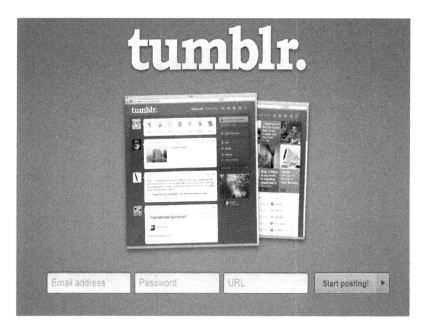

An example of a key word–rich domain for a florist is "flowerarrangments.tumblr.com," or, for a radio reseller, "bargainradios.tumblr.com." The idea is to embed your primary key word or phrase in the URL. This will increase your chances of ranking well on major search engines.

When you've chosen a title, fill in the required information and click the "Start posting" link.

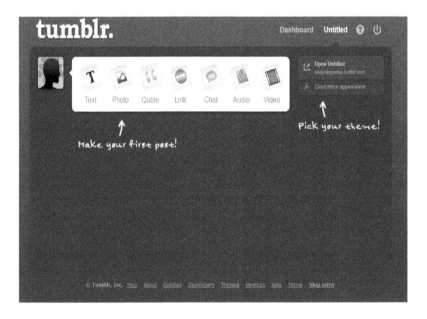

Tumblr is so easy to use that with one click in the dashboard, you can create a blog post. With few more clicks, you can upload a video. Tumblr provides quick access to key posting features.

Let's look at each of the features and how they are used to create quality content for your blog.

Types of Tumblr Posts

Text

Text. The simplest and most frequently used post type on Tumblr is a text post. By clicking on the text icon, you can easily create a text-based post. This is how many traditional posts begin. To create an engaging post, use original content and incorporate key words that are important to you and your audience.

Photo

Photo. Photo blogging is becoming more popular, and Tumblr makes it easy. Photographers can use the platform to showcase their talents. In a photo-based post on Tumblr, you can upload an image and enter a short caption.

Quote

Quote. Blogs are often used as personal diaries or to report things that others have said. With a quote-based post, you can share a quote and its source, as well as a brief description of what you are sharing and why. This feature is unique to Tumblr and is a great way to start a conversation.

Link

Link. Blogs are a great medium for sharing information. Creating a link post is as simple as copying and pasting a URL and selecting a title. If you find valuable content somewhere else on the world wide web, don't be afraid to share it. It's always recommended to add some commentary to your link instead of leaving a link all by itself.

Chat

Chat. An interesting way to create content is to interview people related to your blog topic. Tumblr allows you to post transcripts in chat form. Some of the most popular posts on Tumblr relay conversations with prominent individuals. Think about important people in your niche.

Consider approaching them and asking for an interview. Share your transcript with your audience.

Audio

Audio. Tumblr enables you to upload audio files to your blog. Whether it's a new song from your favorite band or a podcast about a local sports team, audio posts are an easy way to share sound clips with followers. As your blog grows, you may be asked to do interviews. Make sure you get access to the audio files so that you can post them to your site.

Video

Video. Video blogging, or vlogging, is a popular way of sharing information. Post your favorite videos on your Tumblr blog.

It's a good idea to use as many post types as possible to create a dynamic, engaging blog. You will likely favor only a few of these options, but try to make an effort to utilize each of the post types to help improve your search engine rankings and the amount of time people spend on your site.

Customizing Your Tumblr Blog

Each Tumblr blog is automatically set with a default layout, but it can be customized to your liking. From the dashboard, you can modify things such as the blog description, background color, font, and header and background images.

Advanced users can edit the HTML code that drives the overall appearance of the blog and provides unlimited options for development and customization.

You can also choose to build a custom Tumblr theme with HTML or have a designer create a layout for you. As long as you stay within the Tumblr guidelines, you can create something entirely unique.

Like WordPress and Blogger, Tumblr lets you choose from among a number of dynamic themes. These themes change the aesthetic layout of your blog and allow for personalization. Choose from those available in Tumblr's theme library. Similar to the other platforms we've discussed, you can change the overall look and feel of your blog at any time by changing your theme.

The key is to find a theme that meets your specific style and the goals you have for your blog. If you want a customized layout, look for a freelancer who can help you program in HTML. Later in the book, we'll give you some tips on finding freelancers and outsourcing partners who can help with this type of work.

Adding Content Contributors

If you manage your blog with other people, you can add them as members. From the right navigation bar, invite someone to contribute to your blog through e-mail. It's quick and simple.   Once they accept your invitation, they are noted as a content author and can access your blog for posting.

Content Management

Another great feature of Tumblr is the ability to create posts as drafts and then publish them at specific times. Click on the queue tab in the right navigation menu and select when you would like to push your posts live. This is an extremely effective time management tool. Instead of writing one post per day, you can write a few at a time and set them to publish whenever your readers are most active.

Tumblr as a Social Network

One of the best things about Tumblr, besides being an easy tool to use, is that it doubles as a social network. Similar to following people on Twitter or becoming a fan on Facebook, you can follow different blogs on Tumblr. Updates from followed blogs will appear on your dashboard, which makes it easy to repost photos, videos, and more. From the dashboard, you can repost content you find interesting or relevant to your audience. Reposting is a great way to add content to your site quickly and easily. Click on the repost link in the upper right corner of the post you'd like to publish. Reposting makes it easy to spread the word about your blog or business. If you have a large network on Tumblr, you have a good chance of your followers helping you publicize your business or site through reposts. The more people see it, the more likely it is to spread.

How Can You Use Tumblr?

Tumblr is often used differently than Blogger or WordPress. Tumblr bloggers tend to post shorter, more off-the-cuff missives. While many businesses use WordPress and many professional bloggers use Blogger, people who use Tumblr tend to be interested in sharing their latest photos, posting videos, and ranting about politics or their favorite team. Blogs on Tumblr are generally more personal and tend to reflect an individual rather than a company or brand. If you are looking for a blogging tool to share funny pictures, write about fashion, or just speak you mind, Tumblr may be the best option for you.

Think about each of the blogging platforms we've shared with you and consider which one can best meet your needs. By looking closer at the functionality available with each blogging platform and considering your blog-related goals, can you choose a platform that meets your immediate and long-term needs? The time to select and "go" is now.

As noted earlier in this book, the best place to start is with real world experience. After reading this last chapter you should have a better sense of the pros and cons of each blogging platform. If you haven't already done some, create an account on each and begin working with each one.

After a short while, you'll know which platform is the right one for you.

Chapter 4

Managing Your Blog

By now, you've chosen a theme and set up a blog on one of the platforms we've discussed. What's next? Creating valuable content for your audience is the cornerstone of successful blogging and should be where you spend the majority of your time. Although you don't have to create all of the content on your own, it really is the heart and soul of your blog. You can have all the widgets in the world, but unless you're sharing valuable information, you'll never build a loyal audience. Quality content is also essential for monetizing your blog and expanding your reach.

Developing Content

I'm often asked how I come up with ideas for blog posts. The answer is quite simple—I blog about whatever's on my mind that is relevant to my audience. I also look for ways to integrate guest posts and original content from others. I might be reading a news article, having a marketing debate with a colleague, or reading e-mails from followers and suddenly get an idea. I keep a scratch pad handy and jot down any topics appropriate for a blog post.

If you keep a list of ideas handy, it becomes easy to start drafting posts. Sometimes posts don't even start with an idea but rather a video, picture, quote, or audio file. I often bookmark different things I'm reading online or seeing on the web that I want to share with my audience on "The Marketing Blog."

Evernote, a cloud-based note-taking tool, helps me keep track of anything that may serve as the basis for future posts. Regardless of the tool you use, an online notepad, or a scratch pad on your desk, have a place to jot down ideas regarding topics you'd like to cover on your blog.

Another approach is to think of the people you will reach with your blog as friends. After all, they're interested in many of the same things you are. Why else would they be reading your blog? By thinking about your blog readers in this way it becomes easier to identify topics that will engage them.

I've discovered that incorporating different forms of media (text, pictures, and video, for example) dramatically improves reader engagement and even search engine optimization. Google indexes many kinds of assets, thanks to universal search. In fact, Google indexes blog posts, too—especially those that are lengthy, filled with great information, and include multimedia. It's a balancing act. You don't want your blog to load slowly or be cumbersome to navigate due to large graphics or video files. However, the more you jazz up your posts with occasional videos, bold headlines, bullet points, and images, the more engaging it becomes.

Duplicate Content

Original content is essential for successful blogging. Duplicate content—information that's already been published online by a different source—can severely impact your blog's search engine ranking. You may think that copying and pasting someone else's content is an easy way to create posts, but it will damage your ranking and online reputation. If you take nothing else away from this book, remember not to duplicate content. Google has been penalizing sites that publish recycled material for years.

Many people are reluctant to believe it, but I know from years of experience that once Google is aware that your content is not unique, it is much less likely to award your site with any authority. If all you're doing is publishing content from another author, then that author has the authority, not you.

Don't be concerned about how you will generate original content. We will provide a number of extra resources you can refer to in addition to developing your own. At this point in the process, it's more important that you understand the need to develop fresh, original work that only appears on your blog or is published on your blog prior to being published elsewhere. This is vital for improving website rankings, and as your organic rankings improve, you'll generate more blog traffic.

Keyword Research

Once you have an idea for a post, you may want to consider doing some key word research. This is an especially good idea if you're just starting out and your blog doesn't have a great deal of website authority. By focusing on specific key words and the latent semantic index (LSI) associated with your posts, you can create key word rich content that will be indexed by search engine spiders. The concept of LSI means using a primary key word and secondary key words related to your primary phrase.

The quickest way to do key word research is with Google AdWords's Keyword Tool, which allows you to enter a key word phrase to generate a list of accurate traffic data for the term and its related terms.

I like to find key words that aren't too competitive but still have some advertising competition. If you are using Google AdSense to generate revenue for your blog, you can optimize your earning potential by serving ads in a competitive space (those with high advertising competition). The more competitive the space, the more people pay per click and the more revenue you earn. The AdWords tool shows the advertising competitiveness of each term in its index. Remember that Google serves ads related to content, so if you write about a topic that many marketers want to advertise around, you can earn a nice residual income. We'll cover this in greater detail when we discuss monetizing blogs.

Long-tail key words will help you rank well organically. These key words may receive fewer searches in general, but as you add more posts to your blog, you'll get plenty of traffic. For example, the key words "Wii remote" will be more competitive and will receive more searches than a phrase like "white Wii remote." The latter term may land fewer searches, but it is only moderately competitive compared to very competitive, giving you an opportunity to rank well and earn ad revenue.

Effective key word research is a great deal more involved. Fortunately, tools like *SEMrush* and *Market Samurai* can help. The main takeaway is that you should always do key word research before publishing a post to see how much traffic your primary key word receives and to discover related key words to include. As long as you find a term that receives some traffic, you stand a chance of attracting both targeted blog visitors and generating ad revenues.

Once you've completed your research and determined your target key word phrases, it's time to integrate them into an engaging post. Here are some guidelines to consider as you develop content for you blog post:

- Include your key word phrase in the post title.

- Include your key word phrase in a heading.

- Include your key word phrase in an alt image tag.

- Include your key word phrase in the first and last twenty-five words of your post.

- Boldface your key word phrase within the post, if possible.

- Include two or three related key words in your post.

- Don't overstuff your post with keywords (try for a keyword density of between 2 – 4%)

As long as you follow these basic guidelines, you'll give search engines information about the focus of your post. Proper integration of key words helps to improve site authority, rankings, traffic, and, over time, your readership will improve. An optimized post is essential to generating targeted organic traffic.

Creating Dynamic Posts That Engage Readers

It's time to begin writing. An effective post is usually between three hundred and eight hundred words, but it can be of any length. After all, you control the content published on your blog.

In addition to key word integration you'll want to improve your posts with headings, boldface text, bullets, images, videos, and tags.

By making your posts easy to read and engaging, you can increase the average time readers spend on your blog. This is essential for generating repeat visits—a key metric for evaluating the success of your site. Every good post starts with a basic outline. Create an outline that incorporates the points you want to make and the evidence you have to support them. If you're an experienced writer, use your writing skills to draw users in, educate them, and encourage them to take action.

Strong Headlines

The most frequently read posts are those with a strong headline. Think about what draws your attention. The decision to engage with content is largely driven by how a headline resonates with the prospective reader. To that end, spend plenty of time testing different headlines and be sure to include your key word phrase when you craft your post.

Some people have great success with provocative headlines. For example, the most popular post on my blog for the past thirty days is titled <u>7 Strategies For Effective No-Cost Marketing</u>. By using a number in the headline and focusing on something that many people in my niche are interested in, the title taps into reader's curiosity and interest.

In time you can easily see which of your posts acquire the most traffic. Try to duplicate the most effective headlines with slight variations to build on previous successes. Another recommendation is to keep your headlines short. Many blogging platforms use headlines to build post URLs. Shorter URLs tend to do better in search engine rankings when they contain a key word phrase and little else. Try headlines that are short and sweet. The old motto of less is more certainly holds true when creating titles for your posts.

Use Headings and Bullets

Boldface text and bullets dramatically improve the speed at which copy can be read. Always keep readability in mind. Is it easy to scan your post? Can readers acquire the key concepts without reading every word? As you write your post, think of the main idea and supporting points you want to highlight. These should be represented with headings and bullet points. Variations in format improve readability and build loyal followers.

Only highlight key concepts with headings. I like to include key words in headings to provide more weight to the term and help with SEO. Additionally, it signals the reader as to the main objective of the bullet points to follow. Well-formed, concise headings are useful for breaking up content and calling attention to your main ideas.

Bullet points help simplify complex topics and streamline important ideas. They make it easy for readers to scan your text and improve the overall impact of your posts.

Beginning, Middle, and End

This may seem obvious, but blog posts should have a clear beginning, middle, and end. I like to tell readers what a post is about right up front. Why should they have to read through several paragraphs before they figure out what type of information is being shared? If you present your main ideas clearly at the start of a post, the rest will flow. In the middle of the post, provide evidence for your statement, use facts and figures, and include bullet points and anything else you can find to effectively explain your idea. Finally, summarize your post. You may even add a call to action for your readers.

Create posts that stand on their own. Don't expect readers to pick up on prior posts or leave them hanging without a firm conclusion. Ensure that each post presents a complete idea that's well supported. Let your readers know how to use the information you've provided to take the next step.

Images

It's true that a picture is worth a thousand words, and nothing gets the attention of your readers better than an interesting image. As someone who includes a photo with every post, I'm a strong believer that text alone is not enough. There are a number of good resources available for acquiring photos from the Internet. I like to use Creative Commons via Flickr and royalty-free photos from a few different websites. Companies like iStock, and other rights-management photo providers charge for image use. Don't get caught using a photo without permission or attribution. The owner can sue you if the proper permissions have not been granted.

The best way to avoid legal issues is to use royalty-free images as opposed to rights-managed ones. Royalty-free photos do not always require purchase, and if they do, they require only a small, up-front fee. Rights-managed images are very expensive and include a binding agreement that gives you exclusive access for a specified period of time. If you don't want to pay for images, visit Flickr and do an advanced search for royalty-free photos. At the bottom of the search screen, you'll find the option to "only search within Creative Commons-licensed content." There you can find photos that can be used without written consent and without a fee.

The other alternative is to buy a disc of royalty-free photos. You can get dozens of images for about a hundred dollars. Do you research, find photo resources you can depend on, and include them in appropriate posts. You may be able to use thumbnail photos or repurpose existing images. Regardless of the source, avoid rights-managed images—they're not worth the investment for blog-posting purposes.

Videos

It's amazing how pervasive video has become. Now that nearly all computers, tablets, and smartphones have video capabilities, it seems as though everyone and their brother has published video online. Using media for reviews is also very popular. Often posted on YouTube or Amazon, video reviews are generally more engaging than traditional reviews.

Posting videos on your blog can be an effective way to engage people with your content. Videos can improve site interaction and the average time spent on your site. In fact, you can even earn advertising revenue, thanks to YouTube.

If you're new to creating online videos, there's never been a better time to start. Video recorders on smartphones and the software packaged with most computers allow for easy recording. You don't need to be a Hollywood producer—basic videos are simple and effective to both create and publish.

One of my favorite techniques involves publishing videos on YouTube and then embedding them into my blog. This provides a number of benefits:

- There is no need to host a video on your own server.

- It generates traffic from YouTube.

- It provides a channel for generating ad revenue.

- It gives you increased authority for your blog.

By hosting your videos on YouTube, you benefit from their video publishing platform. It is very easy to create a YouTube account, upload a video, and link to the video or embed it on your site. In addition to generating traffic to your blog, you can acquire additional visitors by optimizing your content on YouTube itself which is one of the world's most frequently searched websites. Follow the best practices for search engine optimization on YouTube by embedding key words in your video title and description.

Also create opportunities to encourage reviews, shares, and likes of your video.

Another great feature of using YouTube to host your videos is that through your YouTube account, you can opt-in to participate in the YouTube Adsense advertising program. As readers watch videos on your blog, they may be exposed to advertising related to the content of your video. If they click on an ad, you receive a commission from the ad revenue. You may occasionally want to turn this feature off to limit any possible distractions from the content you're sharing but the choice is entirely yours.

Outsourcing Quality Content

Your blog content should be original for optimization and engagement purposes. Duplicate content will get you into trouble by negatively impacting your search engine rankings and turning off loyal or prospective readers. However, just because content must be unique doesn't mean you have to do all the writing.

I use a number of different techniques to develop original content. Although I like to publish my own posts on a weekly basis, I also like having the flexibility to contribute at my leisure. Here are a few ideas for generating fresh content:

- Partners

- Guest posts

- Freelancers

- Spinning content

If you diversify your content creation strategy, you should have original content flowing your way on a regular basis. Let's look at each of these methods in more detail to help you better understand and evaluate which techniques you prefer.

Partners. A content partner is someone you trust to submit original content on your blog regularly. It could be a friend, coworker, or acquaintance. The benefit of having a content partner is that you can depend on someone to contribute quality content when you need it most. In return, you can provide quality links from your blog back to your partners' website or blog. You may even link to their Google profile, Twitter account, or anything else they are trying to promote in exchange for their contributions.

Another benefit to your partner is the prestige of being a regular contributor. This may seem somewhat trivial, but as your blog gains popularity, others will want to be associated with it. Many blogs have been successful using regular contributors who benefit from the added exposure associated with their contributions.

When you find someone who is knowledgeable in your field and willing to write about what they know, you can use your blog to help build their online reputation and further position them as an expert in their field. This can be a tremendous benefit in exchange for the original content they provide. Choose your content partners wisely. You want them to elevate your presence on the web and support the success of your blog.

It's strongly recommend that you work with content partners to identify key topics that should be covered. Meet with them regularly to discuss upcoming posts, and always read their contributions before publishing them to your blog. Although most blogging platforms allow you to assign multiple authors, I prefer to review posts before they are published. Giving someone full access to your account can cause problems—especially if multiple people are logged into your account at the same time.

Guest Posts. You can't be an expert in everything, and guest posts are an ideal way to provide variety and explore different points of view. Before you invite guests to contribute to your site, consider what type of posts you will accept from others. I like to provide information on my sites about how someone can submit a guest post and the requirements for consideration.

Your instructions should be clear and should define what type of content you'll consider (example below). I also invite sponsored posts, which we discuss in greater detail when we explore monetization.

Example: How to Submit a Guest Post for Sample Blog

Would you like to submit a guest post to "The Sample Blog"? If accepted, you'll be published on one of the world's leading sample blogs alongside other notable marketing experts! We also consider promotional posts.

We are open to new and original content about all things marketing. Before you submit your work for consideration, we ask that you review the following criteria required for a successful submission:

- ***Your content is 100 percent original.*** *Don't waste our time. We aren't interested in previously published work.*

- ***It's gotta be really good.*** *On "The Sample Blog," we pride ourselves on having content you can't find anywhere else. Our readers want practical information they can implement quickly. If you have something that exudes quality, we want it.*

- ***Submissions must be marketing-related.*** *It may seem obvious, but you'd be surprised at the range of content we receive. We love ideas about traditional marketing, online marketing, search marketing, and social media, but anything marketing-related will do.*

- ***Write for our specific audience.*** *"The Sample Blog" caters to people doing business online. This includes small business owners, marketing professionals, affiliate marketers, and fellow bloggers.*

- *Your content must provide value.* There are no minimum word requirements, but your post should be as long as it needs to be—and not much longer than that. I haven't seen quality content that's more than eight hundred or nine hundred words. This is a good rule of thumb.

- *You must be previously published.* In our experience, contributors who have published articles or online content in the past tend to provide quality content. As such, you must have a minimum of three references to online content. Please note that we do not accept articles featured on article distribution websites. Your content must have been published on other noteworthy blogs or websites.

If you have an idea and would like to submit a post, here are the steps to follow for consideration. Submission does not guarantee that your post will be added to the site. Our editors review and approve each post.

1. Read our blog, including our most popular posts. *Doing so will give you an idea of the type of content we publish on "The Sample Blog."*

2. Send us an e-mail about your idea. *Send an idea rather than a finished, polished post. Our editors will approve the idea or suggest changes. Editors for "The Sample Blog" usually respond with two to three business days. If you're ready to submit an idea, please use the Sample.com contact form.*

3. Write the post and submit it for review. *Send us your post in a text or Word document. Please proofread your work for spelling and grammar. A number of posts are rejected daily* because of the amount of editing they would require before publishing. Feel free to include in the post one link to your work, to our work, or to other reputable resources. We like links as long as they're relevant and add value to your piece.

4. Be ready to make revisions. Once we've seen the post, we'll approve it for publication or request revisions. If we request revisions, it isn't an outright rejection of your content. Rather, we want to work with you to make sure that your work is as good as it can be.

5. Plan to participate. We want our authors to interact with reader comments. The day your post goes live and for a few days following, we'll look to you for interaction and feedback. Our audience likes accessibility and hearing directly from our authors.

6. Do your part to promote your post. Have Facebook fans? Twitter followers? We ask our authors to post links to their post using social media.

PROMOTIONAL POSTS

If you would like one of the editors of "The Sample Blog" to review your product or service, contact us using the link below. We never promote a product we haven't tried, and we require a fee for our reviews.

That's it. If you've read the instructions and are still interested in posting to one of the world's top sample blogs, we'd love to add you to our list of marketing experts. If you have any questions or want to send us your idea now, contact us here.

By clearly defining the type of content you'll accept, you avoid pointless e-mails requesting guest posts from individuals who aren't experienced in your niche or have never written a blog post. Publish your guidelines in a prominent area of your blog so they are easy to find. If you receive inquiries from prospective bloggers, point them to your guest post guidelines page. When you have quality guest content coming in on a regular basis, it certainly eases the burden of content creation.

Freelancers. There are hundreds of good writers who are jumping at the chance to write original, quality content for your blog. Although freelancers aren't "free," they are probably less expensive than you might imagine. Keep in mind that there's always a benefit to buying in bulk.

I like to use resources such as *oDesk* and *Freelancer.com* to find experienced writers who can supplement my other content generation strategies. To be honest, this strategy requires a bit of trial and error until you find a resource you can trust. I've hired and fired a number of individuals who claimed to be good writers only to find that their quality was lacking. The good news is that you can try out freelancers for five or ten dollars a post. It's a small investment when you consider the benefits of using a freelancer to generate quality content.

Once you have found reliable freelancers, you can focus on other things, such as monetizing your blog. As long as you have original, quality content, your site can generate revenue, build your online reputation, and grow your business.

Spinning Content. To generate fresh ideas on a small budget, we recommend spinning your own content. If you've never heard of spinning content before, it's a pretty simple concept. Essentially, you take existing content and integrate variables to change certain words or phrases. For example:

I like to {run|walk|jog} at least {two|three times} per week to keep myself {healthy|in good shape|physically fit}.

When this copy renders, multiple variations of the same sentence will appear with random use of one of the words in each bracket. Spinning your content provides multiple versions of the same sentences, which keeps the main idea intact but the copy unique. Unique content is the name of the game when it comes to improving readership and search engine rankings.

Our advice is to use tools like The Best Spinner to quickly and easily spin your posts. You stand the best chance of creating truly unique posts that are more than 40 percent original if you use a well-established spinner with a large database of terms. Forty percent original content should be your minimum target when spinning blog posts to avoid duplicate content penalties from prominent search engines.

You can also use quality content from other open sources, but avoid using someone else's work. There are copyrights and other protections in place to protect original work on the Internet. Your best bet is to have a freelance author generate a variety of posts for you and then get extra mileage from them through spinning.

By using any or all of these techniques for generating content, you can either spend a lot or a little time developing valuable content to share with your audience. We recommend exploring each of these techniques as you may choose to specific techniques at different times during your blog publishing career.

Monetizing your Blog

One of the most exciting aspects of owning and running a blog is generating revenue. Whether you're using your site to produce direct revenue or as a platform to generate leads for products, services, or solutions, you'll find plenty of people who can benefit from your slice of the market.

In this section we share strategies for monetizing blogs. Once you've populated your posts with original content, built a following, and begin appearing in search engine result lists, you're ready to benefit financially from your work.

Even though the topic of generating revenue from blogs is often the one people ask us about most, we've waited until now to introduce moneymaking methods because without the proper understanding of how to create a good blog, most income-generating strategies simply won't work. Your blog has to speak to your niche, generate ample traffic, and be easy to navigate. Once you can cross those items off your list, you're ready to start generating revenue through multiple techniques.

Keep in mind that some monetization methods require more traffic than others. Even if you aren't yet generating the level of traffic you hope to one day receive, put your monetization methods in place now. As your traffic builds, so will your revenue.

What follows is a summary of key strategies for generating revenue from your blog. Before jumping in, keep in mind that every blog is unique. Some of these income streams will work on some blogs better than others. The goal should be to focus on two or three primary revenue drivers and test additional ones as your blog grows. Determine which strategies work best for you and build upon them.

AdSense. AdSense is amazing in terms of its simplicity and earning power. If you haven't already opened a Google AdSense account, what are you waiting for? It's one of the easiest ways to earn money online and it takes just a few minutes to set up. The blogging platforms we've explored offer plugins for displaying AdSense ads— making it even easier to get started generating ad revenue from your blog.

You'll have to experiment with the location and size of your ads to optimize your earning potential without your site appearing cluttered or full of spam. The good news is that Google manages the ad serving for you, so most ads are relevant to the content that surrounds them.

We like to incorporate image and text-based ads, and we have determined that two-hundred-and-fifty-by-three-hundred-pixel ads and two-hundred-by-two-hundred-pixel ads work best for us. Google's blended design tool picks up on the colors used in your blog template and applies them to the ad unit being served. This makes the ads fit seamlessly with your design.

When setting up your ad units, name each placement individually. This will help you monitor and track which ads are getting the most clicks and can lead to further optimization of ad revenue. Google AdSense provides some guidance on the best placement for ad units and how many you should include on your site. AdSense provides a lot of flexibility in terms of incorporating ads of different sizes and formats.

Affiliate Programs. There are hundreds of affiliate programs available that enable you to profit from selling other people's products online. This is ideal for anyone who wants to earn a sales commission without managing fulfillment, customer service, or returns. I promote a variety of affiliate programs on my blogs, creating an ongoing revenue stream of commissions without my ever having to deal with inventory, shipping, or billing. Each month I receive a commission check in my online bank account for the products purchased through my blog.

The most effective affiliate programs are those which are most popular among your audience. I like *Clickbank Marketplace* products that have a high gravity. The concept of gravity is exclusive to the Clickbank affiliate platform and is a measure of a product's sales history and commission payout. The higher the gravity rating, the more popular the product is within the Clickbank platform.

Many top-rated affiliate products sell themselves. It's always a good feeling when a blog reader thanks you for making them aware that a product designed to meet their needs actually exists and where they can find it.

Choose affiliate programs based on your niche. Do some research into the popularity of the product and its commission payout. After promoting many affiliate products with different payout levels, I feel that any product that results in a commission under thirty dollars just isn't worth promoting. If the product you'd like to promote is popular and has a sufficient payout, share in a post or consider adding the product image or promotion to a widget on your blog.

One common way to promote an affiliate product in a blog post is with a product review. Some affiliate programs offer templates for reviews or provide access to the product to try. If the manufacturer has a drafted some type of review for you, remember to spin the content so that your post is original. This is essential for generating organic traffic. You should also carefully consider the title of your post. When others are searching for the product online, there's a good chance that your post will show up in the results. Consider adding a bonus if someone makes a purchase through your blog. This added incentive can improve conversions.

e-Book Sales. Informational products are an effective way to earn revenue from your blog. Although the process of selling e-books can be a little more complicated (such as securing your e-book for download, for example), the benefits are many. Not only can you earn an income from selling your e-book directly, but you can also embed product recommendations that are tracked affiliate links. That way, you generate additional revenue through affiliate commissions if someone clicks through and purchases a product.

While e-books themselves typically retail for under twenty dollars, sales can add up. In fact, in some months, e-books might be one of your biggest sources of income. This income stream grows as you add more e-books that are targeted to your audience and meet their changing needs.

There are a few things to consider when creating and selling an e-book. The first step is to create an e-book that addresses a specific need. Combined with a provocative headline, quality content creates value in the mind of the customer. Start with a solid outline that covers all of the main points you wish to convey. If there are areas of your e-book that are difficult to write, consider using private label rights (PLR) content, available across the Web. For a small fee, usually less than ten dollars, you can use private-label content in this and other works. Although I don't recommend creating an e-book from PLR content alone, it is a good way to begin and e-book publishing strategy.

The next step is to find a cover designer. You'll also need the designer to develop an ad to place on your blog to promote the ebook. Check resources like oDesk to find freelancers to help with the design and development involved in publishing your e-book.

The final step is to use a publishing platform like Digioh or 1shoppingcart to secure your digital assets. Even if you use something simple like PayPal to accept payments, you'll need to find a way to secure your intellectual property so that it isn't shared without your consent.

I recommend conducting additional research on e-books if you plan to use them as a revenue source for your blog. If you can cultivate a list of loyal followers, they'll be anxious to read any additional information you give them. Even if you offer your e-books at a low cost, consider how you can get the most mileage from them with up-sells and affiliate sales. Try to drive purchasers to a secure area of your site to access special offers, bonus content, and more. Consider your e-book an asset that can work for you while you sleep.

Paid-for-Posts and Links. The concept of paid-for-posts is quite simple. Someone contacts you asking for a link to his or her website or product. These requests come more frequently as blogs grow in size and popularity. Before you entertain an advertising or reciprocal relationship with a prospect, be clear on what they want to promote. It's easy to get caught up in the idea that someone wants to pay you to promote his or her service. However, you must always think about your audience. If the product or service is something they would object to, then no amount of money is sufficient and you should let the potential partner know that your blog is not a good fit for their products. As part of any initial review, consider the following options:

- **Option 1:** *A guest post.* Based on the popularity of your blog, you can charge anywhere from twenty dollars to two hundred dollars for a guest post. Whether you write the post or the advertiser submits original content, the concept is the same. You publish a post that focuses on a subject related to the advertiser and embed up to two do-follow links with the anchor text they specify. Do-follow links are links that search engines can view and utilize, passing website authority back to the advertiser. Because you are offering valuable links, try to limit them to one or two. This reduces the amount of link juice you pass to a third party while providing sufficient value for them. Let your advertiser know that the do-follow links will remain active for as long as you manage the blog.

- **Option 2:** *A blogroll link.* Most blogs have a link list. The concept is that advertisers pay you on a monthly basis to have their link listed in your blogroll. Again, keep your outbound links limited so that you're not giving away all of your link authority in exchange for a few bucks. I like to set up PayPal subscriptions to manage billing and payments. The benefit to the advertiser is that he or she can cancel at anytime. As soon as you receive a notice of cancelation, you can delete the link. I charge between twenty dollars and thirty-five dollars a month to host a link on my blogroll.

A great resource for advertisers and link partners is text-link-ads.com. This site acts like a broker to bring together advertisers and publishers—people who have sites that take advertising and people who want to get a message out or build inbound links to their own sites. Visit the text link ads site and register as a publisher. When text-link-ads.com has advertisers seeking placement on blogs such as yours, a notification is sent for your review. If you accept the advertiser, text-link-ads.com provides a URL as well as information about the monthly payout for promoting the link.

Continuity Programs. With a continuity program, you earn a recurring income from people who subscribe to a service you offer. If you don't have your own program to promote, you can promote third-party continuity programs to earn commissions.

Although continuity programs are really a subset of affiliate programs, they are their own animal. When you find a continuity program that fits within your niche, give serious consideration to how you might promote it.

A number of continuity programs are created to deliver ongoing information or create a sense of community among blog readers. One of the best ways to get a handle on continuity programs is to research membership websites in your niche. Membership sites charge a monthly fee that ranges from five dollars to ninety-seven dollars a month. In turn, these sites offer quality content, software, or other resources. Although small numbers of people may drop out of your program each month, others join, which keeps your online revenue stream active. Blogs can be used as the platform for membership programs or to promote them.

Seriously consider continuity programs if you want to make a living online. There are plenty of success stories out there. With the flexibility of WordPress and other platforms, creating a membership site is easier than ever. When you promote membership sites, you receive commissions month after month. When you promote and sell an affiliate product, you make a single commission. Which would you rather have? I love the idea of selling once and earning commissions for as long as that person remains in the continuity program.

Private Ad Sales and Lead Generation. Selling private ads directly is a good way to generate revenue, even though it's not as lucrative for blog owners as it once was. My success with generating online income is largely due to the ability of advertisers to target my blog through Google AdWords. Advertisers don't need to buy ads through me to appear on my site. Because I'm already displaying Google ads, they can go through the Google ad network and target my site specifically.

It's not uncommon to receive e-mails from advertisers asking to buy ad space on your site. Based on the type of advertising you allow, you may be able to accommodate a single advertiser or multiple advertisers. Display advertising is still very much alive, and selling ad space on your virtual real estate can earn you some extra cash. Use tools like Compete.com, Alexa, or your own blog stats to help determine the value of your advertising space—which is directly correlated to "eyeballs." The more traffic you have, the more you should charge for advertising space.

The other opportunity related to ad sales is lead generation. Online colleges and other vendors are constantly looking for new sources of leads. In the online education space, a lead can be incredibly valuable, and I've had schools offer between forty dollars and one hundred dollars per qualified lead. Lead generation is a bit more involved, but can be as simple as placing an ad on your blog or promoting via a guest post. There are also lead generation aggregators in many niches. These are companies that generate leads using affiliates and then sell those leads to the highest bidder.

If you can find a lead aggregator in your niche that is eager for new lead sources, consider how you can leverage your blog to promote it.

Other Ad Networks. *Chitika* and *Bizo* are alternatives to Google AdSense. Chitika delivers relevant ads by targeting search engine results to ensure that users interested in the content see the right advertisements. This greatly increases the chance that users will click on ads, maximizing your earning potential. Although I've focused less on Chitika and Bizo, their ads tend to perform well and generally have a higher payout.

Keep in mind that all aggregators work differently. To get a feel for how they function, watch online demos or contact a representative. They can't promise how much you will earn, but they can provide an estimate based on other customers in your niche. Implementing ad code on your site is fairly simple but does require a programmer unless you're familiar with HTML and JavaScript.

When starting a new program, give it two to three weeks before you make an evaluation. The algorithms need to evolve before they start serving ads that result in higher click-through rates and more commission.

Amazon Associates. The Amazon affiliate program has become a major source of revenue for Internet marketers. The beauty of Amazon is that if you promote a product on your site and a prospect buys an alternative product from Amazon after clicking on your link, you earn a commission. Amazon has a number of tools for affiliates, making it easy to promote a huge range of products.

To become an Amazon affiliate, visit the <u>Amazon affiliate center</u> and register. Search for products you'd like to promote and access links and other resources to place on your site. You can even add an Amazon widget or an entire Amazon store customized for your audience. The program is so flexible that not becoming an affiliate is silly. Payouts average at 4 percent of each purchase, but commissions vary. Even though I don't use Amazon widgets on all my blogs, I regularly incorporate Amazon affiliate tools into posts, resulting in product specific commissions.

A really good use of Amazon affiliate links is for seasonal promotions. For example, near Halloween, you can direct individuals to Amazon to purchase costumes by sharing your own or posting a picture. In the lead-up to Valentine's Day, link to gifts and accessories from your posts. It may seem like a small initiative, but over time, your blog can host a range of moneymaking links to valuable goods. Be conservative and mindful of the opportunities you have to connect people with the merchandise they're already looking for.

Consulting and Speaking Fees. Once you build authority for your blog, others will seek you out for consulting and speaking engagements. Although I don't proactively look for speaking opportunities on my own, I am contacted a number of times each year to speak in front of audiences (at trade shows, for businesses, and so on). When you're asked to share your expertise, consider doing the presentation at no cost. Think about monetizing your listeners during and after the speech. In other words, always have the long term in mind. As long as you're reimbursed for travel, consider yourself ahead of the game and the opportunity at your fingertips.

What's nice about blogging is that you can leverage your online presence offline. Once you start giving presentations or interviews, you can promote yourself to gain even more followers. Interviews and speaking engagements add credibility to you and your blog.

Always ask for a recording of your presentation. If the organization you're working with does not offer to record your speech, purchase an inexpensive app for your smartphone, iPad, or computer that can do the job for you. Even if audio is all you capture, it can be repackaged and distributed on your blog. I know a lot of Internet marketers who generate a good deal of revenue by repackaging content they have already produced in a different format.

Personal Coaching. Once you have started a blog and built your knowledge across a particular platform, others may be interested in having you help them set up their blogs or teach them how to run a successful site. Consider providing one-on-one coaching or holding webinars to teach people the benefits of blogging. Promote your coaching services on your own blog and through any lists you build. Many people make a living off coaching others on how to build successful online programs. In fact, a number of individuals I work with in the Internet marketing niche now charge more than $300/hr. for one-one one coaching. This comes with time but is certainly attainable.

The Power of the List. We've referred to list creation throughout this book but haven't yet explored the concept in depth. Of all the things you can do on a blog, creating a list of followers is one of the most important for generating revenue. Once you acquire a name and contact information, you can market to these individuals directly. Don't get me wrong—I'm not talking about sending out useless emails or spam. Rather, you'll be providing quality information your followers want and can benefit from.

Here are some basic guidelines for effective list building:

- Use an auto responder such as Aweber to seamlessly manage follow-up e-mails, opt outs, and so on.

- Evolve your list-building techniques (with test incentives and pop-ups, for example).

- Don't send mail too frequently. Once or twice per month is enough.

- Always follow CAN-SPAM laws, such as providing a ten-day opt-out period and including your physical address in your e-mails (Aweber manages most of this for you).

Over time, lists can become incredibly valuable. Begin with some basic opt-in lists and evolve your techniques over time to build an effective list.

New revenue generation techniques emerge every day for blog owners. Begin today by choosing one or two methods we've covered and let them run their course. You never know if something is going to work unless you give it your full attention. Once you have a primary revenue driver, try adding other sources of revenue such as e-books, affiliate programs, and so on. You can quickly build a recurring revenue stream that others will envy.

For many bloggers, making money is important, but it's not the primary goal. No matter what you use your blog for, however, generating income can be ideal for investing in upgrades, additional features, and improving your reach.

Outsourcing

Now that you know how to launch a blog, create content, and monetize your traffic, it's time to talk about maintenance. This is an essential part of any successful blog and often means the difference between a flourishing site and one that simply withers away.

The concept of outsourcing is not new. The term *outsourcing* is generally used to refer to a business function that an outside vendor or freelancer is paid to provide. You may have also heard the term *offshoring*, which refers to using outsourcing partners located outside of your own country.

One of the biggest trends in recent years is the increase in individuals using online technology to outsource, allowing them to build viable businesses that can be run from anywhere in the world. A primary motivation for sourcing freelancers from other countries is that you can purchase services for pennies on the dollar. I've purchased work from highly qualified individuals for as little as three dollars per hour.

Outsourcing is especially effective for creating websites, programming code, or providing marketing support functions. All elements can be done remotely and delivered digitally. Service providers can leverage the scale and economy of outsourcing to deliver high-value services at vastly reduced prices.

Finding an Outsourcing Partner

Does the idea of finding an affordable, qualified professional to help you achieve your blogging goals appeal to you? If so, the first step is to register for a network that provides access to freelancers and companies that offer low-cost outsourcing services.

The good news is that with the popularity of do-it-yourself websites, blogs, and other online media, it is easy to find a source for qualified talent. After having used outsourcers for almost a decade, I can tell that finding the right outsourcer takes a bit of work but is definitely worth it in the end.

We all have a preferred style of working and managing others. To that end, finding the best fit can be like finding a needle in a haystack. There are a few websites that make the matching process relatively straightforward, easing the burden on people like us looking for a qualified resource

We use two freelance-finding resources exclusively based on my personal needs. The first is oDesk, a huge marketplace for everything from administrative assistants to PHP programmers. This platform is robust enough that you can usually find a qualified provider at the price you're willing to spend.

Get the right contractor. Get the job done.

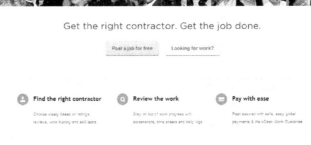

oDesk is great for finding programmers and freelancers to complete simple tasks (for example, to spin articles, add social media buttons to my blog, or conduct online research). If you have a larger project, such as redesigning an entire blog or website, I recommend Elance, which we discuss in more detail shortly.

To use oDesk, register yourself or your business at the oDesk website. Once registered, you can begin your search for a qualified freelancer.

There are essentially two ways to go about finding the right person for the job. The first is by posting a job. You will need to answer a few qualifying questions and describe the work you need done. You can select advanced job requirements around specific criteria. You'll soon receive responses from prospective freelancers who are both qualified and interested in taking on the job you have posted.

Since many freelancers regularly work through oDesk, they may provide generic responses to job postings. This isn't a good thing. You want potential freelancers to read your job posting to determine if they truly qualify. To that end, I've adopted the habit of asking freelancers to respond to my posts with a very specific subject line (for example, "Yellow Cactus"). By requiring freelancers to use a specific phrase in the subject of their response to your job posting, you can quickly sort through the potentially dozens of responses you'll receive. I always look for detail-oriented freelancers so I don't have to check everything they do!

The second way to find a freelancer using oDesk is with an advanced search. You can find candidates based on the type of work they qualify for, their ratings, their test scores, and so on. This is a great tool if you're in a rush and don't want to wait for responses via e-mail. Once you've narrowed down your list, you can send a message to prospective candidates. This allows for some additional screening and can help you find the perfect match.

Once you have awarded the job to a freelancer, you will provide additional details and answer any questions the freelancer might have. When you sign up for oDesk, you provide credit card or PayPal information. As the freelancer logs hours, oDesk calculates the fees owed and will automatically bill to your account weekly.

What I like about oDesk is that you can track your freelancer's progress on the job. The "manage team" feature captures screenshots of your freelancer's computer screen every ten minutes or so. This way you know your freelancer is logging legitimate hours.

Finding the right contractor takes time, so don't be discouraged if you work with a few people who aren't ideal. It took the completion of quite a few small projects before I found someone who delivered precisely what I was looking for and matched my style for speed, detail, and demeanor. I recommend that you test out freelancers on small projects before assigning more significant tasks like fully managing a section of your blog. Think of small, repetitive tasks that are time-consuming but don't generate direct revenue (approving or deleting comments, for example) and let your freelancers start there. By using inexpensive freelancers for mundane tasks that aren't revenue-generating, you can focus on more important tools that grow your business.

Now that we've explored oDesk, let's talk about the second outsourcing network I use to develop websites, landing pages, and blogs: Elance.

Elance brings together more than five hundred thousand rated and tested professionals to fulfill various freelance needs. You can find a variety of candidates for your job, set milestones, and approve all work before you pay.

Elance works much like oDesk. You can search for freelancers or post a job. Either way, with such a large pool of potential providers, you're bound to find two or three solid proposals that are within your price range and meet your criteria.

Again, to optimize your chances of finding the perfect vendor, ask candidates to include something specific in the subject line of their bids and define specific deliverables. Elance predicates payment for vendors according to specific milestones. Milestones help keep a project on track and are typically not used as effectively on other freelance networks.

Keep in mind that you must fund each milestone in advance. You pay up front, and the money goes into an escrow account until you agree to release it to the vendor.

Freelancers and outsourcing companies available through Elance and oDesk could be based anywhere in world. Fortunately these networks manage the particulars so that you can focus on getting your project done. Due to the global aspect of freelancing, we've had high-end websites built for less than $2,500. In the United States, the same work would have cost me $20,000 to $30,000. It's almost funny to get into philosophical debates about hiring international workers versus using homegrown resources. Our cost structures are so out of whack with the rest of the world that Internet marketers and bloggers are foolish not to look at the international development resources available today.

Outsourced Blog Posts

Now that you understand the power of outsourcing and how to go about finding freelancers, the next step is to determine what you really need for your blog and to set up a manageable schedule for keep it all under control. A good question to ask yourself is the following, "If you had unlimited resources, which tasks would you assign to others and which tasks would you do yourself?"

It helps to prioritize the tasks you want to outsource. Moderating comments and writing fresh content can be some of the most time-consuming aspects of managing a blog. Once you find the right person to help with these tasks, you can focus on generating revenue and promoting your site.

If you have trouble finding the right partner to contribute rich, value-added content, consider putting more routine tasks out to outsourcers: uploading posts, moderating comments, and responding to inquiries. Finding someone to generate unique content takes time. Knowing that you can hire help to keep your blog going is a huge relief. As noted earlier, it's a good idea to sample the work of your prospective freelancers. Since your costs are fairly low, test a few different candidates and choose the one you like most.

In addition to using a freelancer, I occasionally invite other people help out. Inviting others to post gives them a chance to publish online and provides me with one or two free original posts per month. When writers make contributions to a popular blog, they usually promote their work. This solves two problems: content development and promotion.

Promoting your Blog

When your blog is positioned for monetization and you're posting valuable content on a regular basis, it's time to turn up the heat in terms of promotion. The primary goal of promotion should be quality traffic versus quantity. This is where many bloggers go wrong. Sure, it's nice to have tons of visits to your blog every day, but if people don't stay on the site very long or return often, you're promotional efforts are practically meaningless. The goal is not to be all things to all people, but rather to build a list of loyal followers who will tell others and drive traffic to your blog.

Free Promotion

Blog Sharing Icons. One of my favorite promotional methods is to incorporate sharing icons. Visit Addthis.com or Sharethis.com and follow the instructions for implementing "share" icons to your site. When users visit your blog, they can click on the icons to link to their favorite social media platforms, such as Twitter, Facebook, or Digg. After entering their username and password, they can post a link to your blog. This helps to create awareness for your blog and build link authority for search engine optimization.

Post Sharing Icons. In addition to incorporating share icons into your blog template, you can also add them to each post. You may think this is redundant, but it's one of the best ways to promote individual posts and take advantage of viral marketing. Blogs that do this well embed Twitter, Google+, and Facebook "like" buttons with every post.

Most of the blog platforms discussed in this book offer plugins for sharing icons. You can control which social media platforms you want to include and update them on a regular basis. Regardless of which method you use to integrating share functionality, be sure to make sharing easy among your blog readers and browsers.

Search Engine Optimization. Ensuring that your blog is properly optimized for search engines is essential for generating organic traffic. When your blog appears at the top of search results for a specific key word or phrase, users are more likely to click through to visit. SEO is not the focus of this book (see *SEO Made Simple* for in-depth search engine optimization advice) but it is essential for growing blog traffic. Always specify your site's meta data including; page title, description, and key words. Apply SEO best practices such using key words in post titles and pages for best optimization. If you do this consistently, you'll build an optimized blog and appear high up in search engine results.

Focus On Content. There are a number of ways that others can help you promote your blog. As mentioned, allowing guest posts and asking authors to share the post (and your blog) with their audiences is a key strategy for driving traffic and increasing awareness.

The same thing happens when you offer original content to another blog within your niche. By submitting a guest post to another site, you are building exposure. Always include a link to your blog in guest posts that you offer to other websites or blogs.

Crowd Sourcing and Social Media. Another strategy to consider is adding Google Friend Connect, Facebook friends, and other "follow" widgets to your blog. When people visit your site and see that others have signed up to receive updates, crowd sourcing takes over—they want to belong to the masses. You will gain followers who return to your blog often and share your links with their networks of friends.

Social media is one of the fastest ways to let others know about your blog and build a foundation of repeat visitors. When social information is evidenced on your site, others see your popularity and want to join.

Always have an eye towards promotion. Too often we've seen blogs with fantastic content that never get noticed. Don't let this happen to you. Make it easy for others to recognize and promote your blog.

Paid Promotion

As is true with any online asset, you can promote your blog with traditional online media: pay-per-click, pay-per-view, rich media, and so on. I've rarely used paid media to promote my blog. However, if you have the money and know the complexities of Internet marketing, try your hand at paid promotion. From my perspective, unless your blog is a moneymaking machine—one that allows you to fully understand your cost and profit per visitor—spending money on advertising does not make much sense.

If you choose to spend money on advertising, my recommendation is to start with Google AdWords. Because it is a highly trafficked advertising network, you can learn a great deal about your audience and the type of people who visit and return to your blog. I also recommend installing Google Analytics to fully track your blog activity and gain valuable insights about your audience.

Don't begin with paid promotions until you have a firm grasp of your cost per acquisition and average revenue per visitor. These metrics are essential to understand before you start spending money. When you know what it costs to get a visitor, and how much revenue that visitor generates, you're in a better position to determine what you should spend. Until then, focus on free promotional methods and build your network of contacts.

Conclusion

We hope you've learned that blogging is not only fun but can be lucrative as well. A wise man once told me that you get out of something what you put into it—and he was right. Blogging can be a casual way to share ideas or a means to promoting your business. It can also be a way to earn money and enjoy the lifestyle you desire.

If you haven't already done so, carefully consider what your blog will be about and your primary goal. Is it to share your expertise or serve prospective buyers of your products or services? Although we can't set your goal for you, we suggest that you stick with what you know and determine how best to create value for others.

Create milestones for your blog. Take the small steps required for getting your site up and running. Once your blog is live, determine how to maintain and build upon what you've created. Setting goals is essential for expanding and growing your blog.

In this book, we introduced a few user-friendly blogging platforms. WordPress, Blogger, and Tumblr each have pros and cons. Consider what you want your blog to look like, the user experience you want to create, and which platform will best meet your needs. Once you start working with your chosen platform, you'll discover that blogging is easy and quite honestly a great deal of fun. That's one of the reasons we wrote this book—to share our passion.

Today's most popular blogging platforms are constantly introducing new features. If you're posting to your blog on a regular basis, you can easily tune in to what's new and apply interesting features to your site. Making updates on a regular basis enriches the experience for your loyal readers. Consider interacting with your blog readers. Let them know of upgrades, changes, and new posts. In addition to building an online asset, you are also building a community.

Blogging is a truly rewarding experience. Not only do you create value for others, but you create value for yourself. Today your goal may simply be to create a blog. In the future, it may be to generate multiple streams of revenue. Regardless of your goal, you must begin.

We encourage you to reread this guide as often as necessary to build and develop your very own blog. Even though blogging continues to evolve, the principals outlined throughout this book are evergreen. We wish you much success with your blogging and look forward to reading your blog!

*****BONUS*****

THANK YOU FOR PURCHASING AND READING OUR BOOK, "BLOGGING MADE SIMPLE."

PLEASE BE SURE TO LEAVE AN HONEST REVIEW ON AMAZON.COM FOR THIS TITLE. WE HAVE PREPARED A SPECIAL BONUS FOR YOU. ONCE YOUR REVIEW IS POSTED, PLEASE NOTIFY US AT SUPPORT@MARKETINGSCOOP.COM

*****BLOGGING HELP*****

Join our growing community of bloggers and Internet marketers at the *SCOOP Marketing Forum.* Visit http://www.scoopmarketingforum.com and join for FREE!